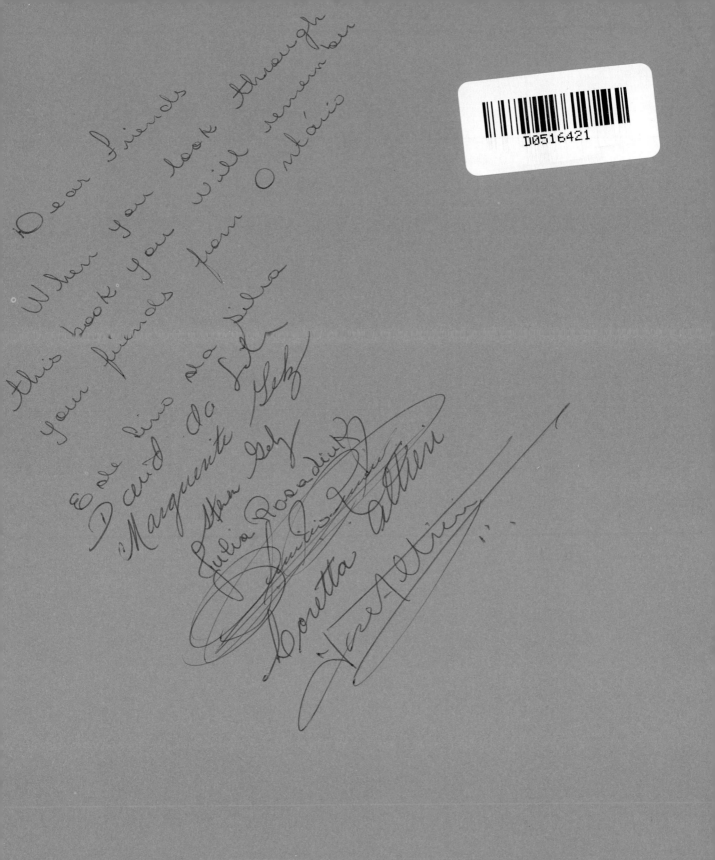

Dear Friends

When you look through
this book you will remember
your friends from Ontario

Else Pinto da Silva
David da Sá
"Marguerite Gehz
Mara Gehz
Julia Rosadius
Lucilia Pereira
Loretta Altieri
Rose Altieri

April, 11, 1981

ONTARIO

A PICTURE BOOK TO REMEMBER HER BY

Designed by
DAVID GIBBON

Produced by
TED SMART

CRESCENT BOOKS
NEW YORK

INTRODUCTION

Ontario is the second largest province of Canada, lying between the Hudson and James Bays to the north, Quebec to the east, the St Lawrence and the Great Lakes to the south and Manitoba to the west. It is also Canada's most populous province, with more than seven million inhabitants, over one third of the country's total, and its natural resources and industrial development have also made it the wealthiest.

Ontario's earliest known Indian dwellers included the Tobacco, Erie and Huron tribes in the south, whose existence was based on agriculture, and the hunting tribes, the Algonquin, Ojibwa and Cree in the harsher climes of the north.

A French explorer, Etienne Brûlé, is believed to have been the first white man to travel among the Indians, on an expedition to the Ottawa River in 1610-11. Before long he was followed by Samuel de Champlain, the acknowledged founder of Quebec, and in his wake came an assortment of other French explorers, fur traders and missionaries. In 1648-49, the southern Indian tribes were driven from their lands as France began to protect her rapidly expanding fur empire.

More than 100 years later, in 1774, the Quebec Act established Ontario as part of an extended colony ruled from Quebec. The following year saw the start of the American War of Independence and Ontario became a base for Loyalist and Indian attacks upon the American frontier. At the end of the war the area was settled by 10,000 of those Loyalists and a number of Iroquois Indians who had fought for the British.

A Constitutional Act of 1791 divided Quebec Colony into Lower Canada, with a French majority, and Upper Canada as a Loyalist province. Upper Canada – now Ontario – adopted the English local government and legal practices, established an Anglican church and chose York – later to be renamed Toronto – as its capital. Upper and Lower Canada were united in 1841, when Upper Canada became known as Canada West, but this name was changed to Ontario a few years later.

Since those days the province has made enormous strides towards a thriving industrial economy, helped initially by the advent of the railways in the 1850's, which established Toronto as a serious commercial rival to the city of Montreal. Other advances were the harnessing of power from Niagara Falls in 1882 and the discovery of minerals such as gold, silver, copper, nickel and iron at the beginning of the 20th century. The expansion of lumbering in the province's extensive forests, and the subsequent paper and pulp industries also helped to put Ontario on a firm economic footing.

The province can be divided into two distinct regions. Northern Ontario is composed of lakes and rivers, dense forests of spruce, pine, balsam and birch, with a band of tundra along Hudson Bay. Southern Ontario, virtually ten percent of the province, contains ninety percent of the population and is the major industrial region, not only of Ontario, but of the whole of Canada. Automobiles, textiles, food processing, aircraft and electrical goods are the main manufacturing industries. This part of the province has several beautiful lake districts and, of course, the spectacular Niagara Falls. Toronto, on the northern shore of Lake Ontario, is Canada's second city and the capital of Ontario. The first known settlement in the Toronto area is believed to have been called Teiaiagon, inhabited by the Seneca and later the Mississauge Indians. In time it became a trading post, and an important one, due to its position at the crossing of ancient Indian trails leading to the north and west; trails that were gratefully used by the early explorers and fur traders.

The name Toronto was given to a small fort, one of three built by the French between 1720 and 1750 in order to defend their trade with the Indians against the English. In 1757 the French were defeated and the forts destroyed, although the settlement at Toronto continued as a trading post. After the massive influx of Loyalists into the province following the ending of the American War of Independence, Lord Dorchester, Governor in Chief of Canada, negotiated with three Indian Chiefs for the purchase of a site for a future Ontario capital. The land chosen was 250,000-acres adjoining Lake Ontario. It was eventually bought for £1,700, bales of cloth, axes and a variety of other goods. Ontario's first parliament, however, met at Niagara in 1792 but a year later the Lieutenant Governor chose the present site of Toronto, impressed by its strategic defensive position, excellent harbour and trading potential. Curiously, he changed its name from Toronto to York, which it remained until 1834, when the city, with a population of about 9,000, was incorporated.

A serious fire in 1849 destroyed fifteen acres of the downtown area including the cathedral and St Lawrence market, but the city quickly recovered. The construction of the Grand Trunk and Great Western Railway in the next decade was responsible for the city's rapid development in industry, trading, distribution and population. In 1861 the population was 45,000; 1901 208,000 and 1921 522,000. However, like many other cities, Toronto suffered during the depression years of the 1930's and an increase in population after World War II only fuelled the problem of finding enough money to finance essential services.

Toronto today is a cosmopolitan metropolis and the commercial powerhouse of the nation. It has expanded along the curving western shoreline of Lake Ontario, from Oshawa to St Catherines; an area known as the Golden Horseshoe. In the city centre clusters of gleaming skyscrapers house the offices of multi-national corporations; concrete symbols of Toronto's affluence.

It is, in addition, the headquarters of the English speaking press and prides itself on its wide range of cultural activities. The Toronto Symphony Orchestra, three major theatres, the Royal Ontario Museum and the Art Gallery of Ontario are just a few of the city's amenities. Here, as well as throughout the province, there are universities and colleges providing excellent educational opportunities and there are everywhere realistic social services.

Toronto and Ontario are still favourite destinations for immigrants from many countries and it is said that a quarter of a million Ontarians speak no English at all. It is no wonder, however, given the opportunities that exist for those prepared to work hard, that so many people have chosen to make their homes in this particular part of Canada.

The modern skyline of Toronto *left and overleaf* reflects the dynamic character of Ontario's capital, the largest English-speaking city in Canada and a major financial, industrial and cultural centre.

The City Hall *below, below right, overleaf* and viewed *above* from the Sheraton Centre is a striking $30 million complex created by the Finnish architect Viljo Revell. Encircled by two arc-shaped towers, the three-story rotunda contains a graceful column, 6 metres in diameter, which serves as a pedestal for the domed amphitheatre of the Council Chamber. The Sheraton Centre *above right* vies with the Bank of Montreal and the Hotel Toronto for the Toronto skyline and the Toronto Harbour Castle Hilton *left* towers over the ships of the city's harbour.

Set on Lake Ontario in front of the
Canadian National Exhibition Grounds,
Ontario Place *on these pages and overleaf*
was constructed as a showplace for the
province and the nation. The complex
which extends over 96 acres consists of
five modules suspended over the lake on
concrete columns 32 metres high, and also
includes winding canals, lagoons, sandy
beaches and a marina *below right* among
parklands rich in attractions such as the
Roller Rink *above right.*
The Cinesphere *above,* one of the most
advanced theatres in the world, shows
technically advanced films on a huge
screen in an auditorium which will hold
800 people.

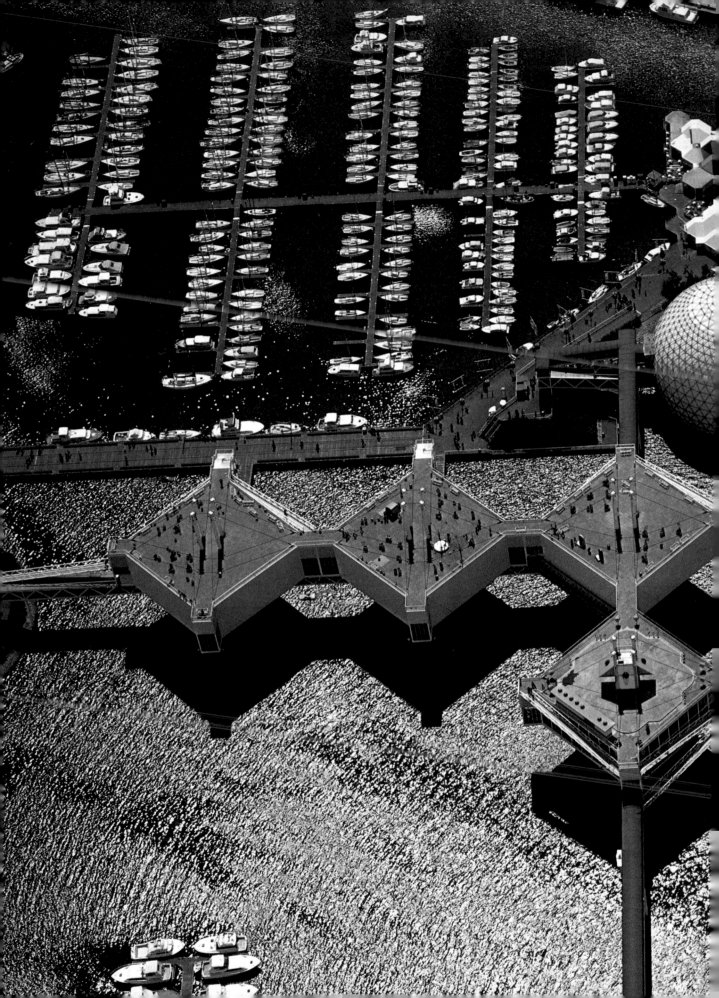

The oldest and largest annual exhibition in the world, the 'Ex' in the Canadian National Exhibition Grounds *on these pages* is a Canadian institution. For over a century it has been held, with a multitude of agricultural and technical exhibits, a large midway, a spectacular water show and a host of other colourful events. At night the CN Tower provides a breathtaking view of the city's illuminated sky-scrapers *overleaf*.

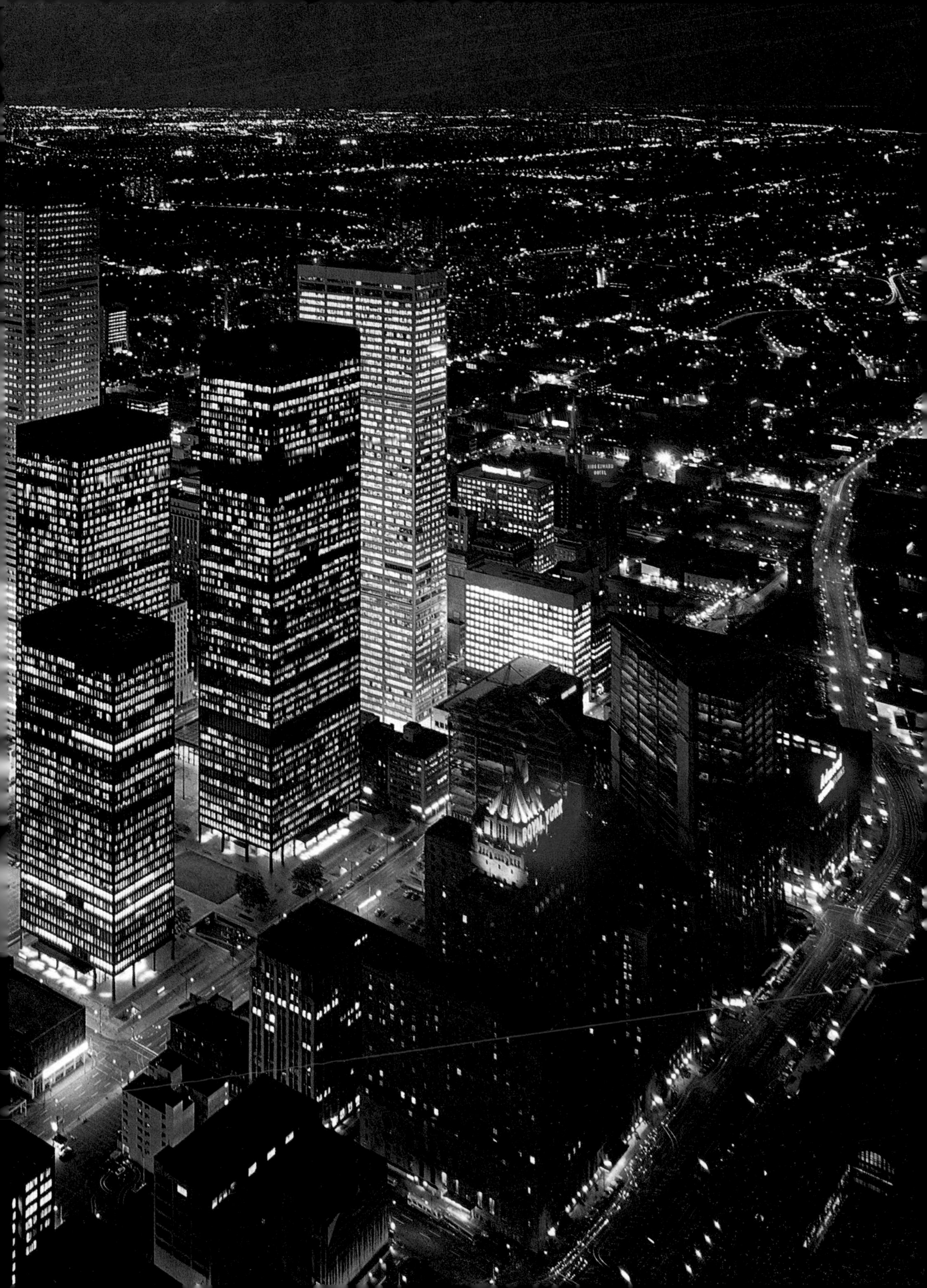
ROYAL YORK

At the foot of John Street stands one of the tallest free standing structures in the world, the C.N. Tower *above and below left* and *above*. Rising to a spectacular height of 533.33 metres, it is designed to provide the world's most efficient facilities for television and radio stations but its observation decks also provide magnificent views of Toronto and its skyline *right*.

Casa Loma *overleaf*, a 98 room mansion, was built between 1911 and 1914 by a Toronto soldier, financier and industrialist. Its secret panels and hidden stairways lend it all the atmosphere of a fairy-tale castle and its turreted stables have floors of Spanish tile and stalls of Spanish mahogany.

Despite the modern face of Toronto with its sophisticated CN Tower *above left*, its New City Hall *below left* and its busy shopping centres such as Yonge Street *right*, the city has retained many reminders of its traditional past. Nathan Phillips Square *above* was named in honour of a former mayor of Toronto who initiated the New City Hall project, a statue of Sir John A. Macdonald, Canada's first Prime Minister overlooks University Avenue *left*, and the Old City Hall *below*, officially opened in 1899, still stands in Nathan Phillips Square.

The Yorkville area *left* and *above and centre right*, which started as a separate village, became part of Toronto in 1883. Today, it has become a pleasant shopping district with numerous sidewalk cafés, among them the attractive Hazelton Café *above* and *below right*.
The neon signs of a Chinese restaurant *below* bring international colour to Elizabeth Street and *overleaf*, a colourful array of food and flowers invites visitors to Fenton's Restaurant.

Toronto has a sizeable downtown shopping district, extending from Yonge Street to University Avenue and from King Street, north to College Street. Eaton Centre on Yonge Street *these pages* first opened its doors in 1977 and must rank among the world's finest shopping areas.

Perhaps the most striking feature of Toronto is its gigantic skyline of hotels, office buildings and tall banks *centre and below right.* Even from the relative tranquillity of the water front *above right,* the city's ever-changing face is dominated by towering commercial complexes bearing the names of Canada's leading banks and one of the most striking of these, the dazzling Royal Bank Plaza *above and left* features twin towers covered with $250,000 in gold leaf. Between the ultra-modern sky-scrapers, the Parliament Buildings *below* are clearly visible at the end of University Avenue.

Kensington Market *on these pages* offers a tempting array of almost any type of fish and meat produce available in the city and a mouthwatering range of the freshest of fruit and vegetables. Visitors to Toronto flock here not only to shop but also to admire and savour the colourful displays and international atmosphere.

In Exhibition Place Stadium the Toronto Blue Jays *this page* of the American Baseball League draw huge crowds of spectators throughout the baseball season. Not far from the city centre, the Metro Toronto Zoo *right* has on its 710 acres thousands of plants and animals from Indo-Malaya, Africa, North and South America, Eurasia and Australia.
The Gothic architecture of the Houses of Parliament in Canada's capital Ottawa, dominates the city and Ottawa River *overleaf*.

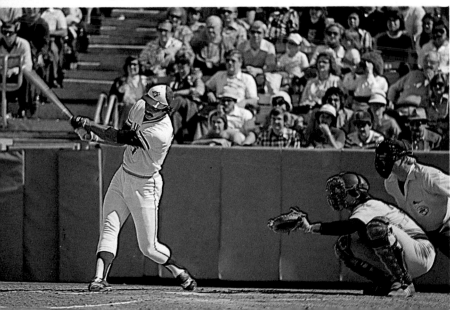

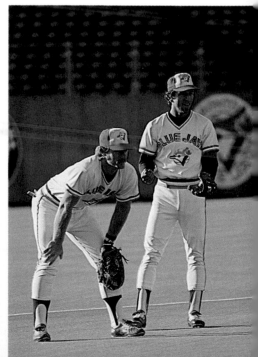

Built between 1859 and 1865, the Houses of Parliament consist of three buildings crowned by the magnificent Peace Tower with its carillon of 53 bells. On the lawns of Parliament Hill, the Changing of the Guard, an ancient military ceremony, is performed by Her Majesty's Canadian Guards *left and right*. Outside Parliament also, an officer of the Royal Canadian Mounted Police is always on duty *above and below* to give help and advice to visitors.

To the right of the Parliament Buildings *overleaf* stands the famous Chateau Laurier, the renowned hotel built of granite and Indiana sandstone.

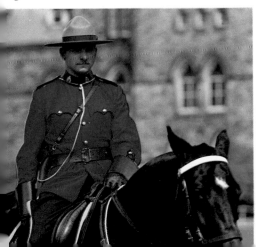

Before the Parliament Buildings *above right* the Centennial flame *below right* burns as a symbol of Canada's 100 years of nationhood, and inside the buildings the Senate Chamber *overleaf* and the Confederation Hall *centre right* are just two of many magnificent rooms.

In Major's Hill Park *left* autumn leaves frame the views across the Ottawa River. The Rideau Canal *below* was completed in 1832, on the advice of the Duke of Wellington, to allow British gunboats to avoid the American cannon on the St Lawrence. Never used for military purposes, it became a commercial waterway and today is used for pleasure-boat cruising in summer and skating in winter.

In Nepean Park, a statue *above* pays tribute to Samuel de Champlain, the French explorer and founder of New France.

Whether in summer *above and below right* or in winter *below left* and *overleaf* the Niagara Falls, where the mighty Niagara River, divided by the international boundary, plunges over the escarpment into a deep gorge, is one of the world's most spectacular sights. The Canadian Horseshoe Falls *above left* and *left*, 54 metres high, have a crest of over 761 metres outlining a deep curve, from which the name 'horseshoe' derives.

To show the falls to their full advantage the Whirpool Aerocar *above* carries passengers high over the Niagara Gorge and the churning Whirpool Basin and the Horseshoe Falls Incline Railway *below* provides twin cable-rail cars between the Panasonic Centre and Table Rock House.

Founded in 1673 by Count Frontenac, Governor of New France, as a fur-trading post and strategic military stronghold, Kingston *on these pages* lies at the point where Lake Ontario empties into the St Lawrence River at the head of the Thousand Islands. Kingston today has retained many of its early landmarks, among them, the City Hall *above and below* which was constructed in 1843–44 while Kingston was the capital of the United Provinces of Canada. Bellevue House *left*, the residence of Sir John A. Macdonald, first prime minister of Canada, was built in 1838. Today the 15 room Tuscan Villa has been restored and furnished to its original state.

Standing on a hill overlooking the city of Kingston, Old Fort Henry *these pages*, originally built during the war of 1812 and rebuilt between 1832 and 1836, has been completely restored as a museum of British and Canadian military history. The 'Fort Henry Guard' trained and uniformed as British troops of 1867, parade daily. Performances include British infantry drill and tactics and salutes are fired daily, using the fort's original muzzle-loading cannon, cast in Scotland between 1794 and 1806.

Not far from Morrisburg, Upper Canada Village *on these pages* is a recreation of a typical St Lawrence Valley community of the 19th century. Approximately 40 buildings, originally destined for inundation by the St Lawrence Seaway, were moved from their original sites to form this memorial to the pioneer settlers of the province and now in many parts of the village men and women may be seen busying themselves over tasks which formed part of daily life in years gone by.

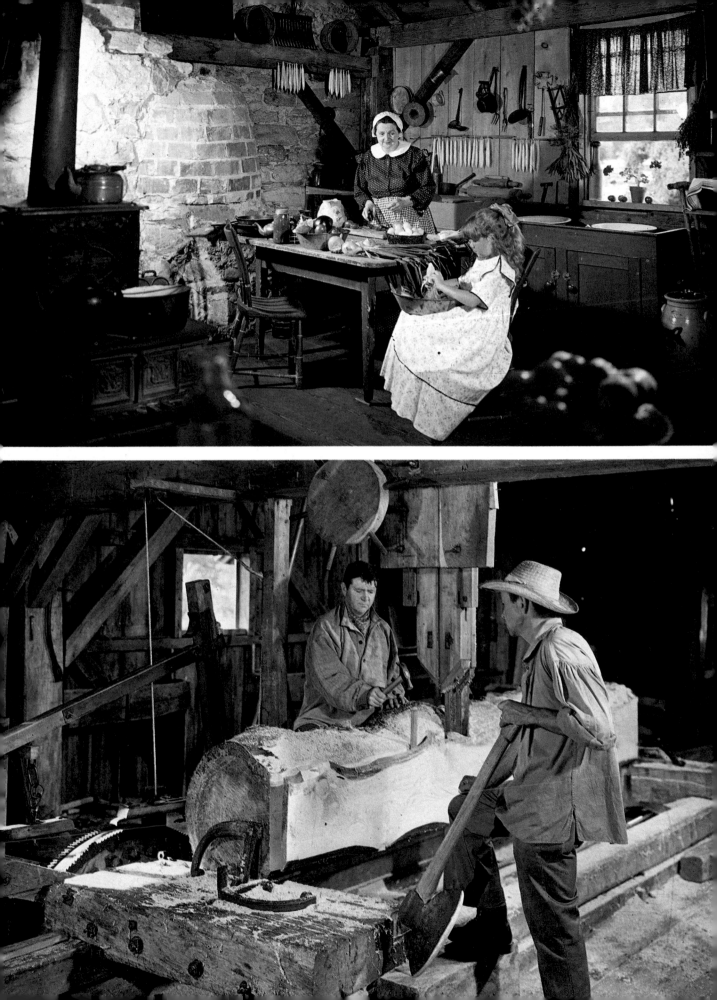

For many Ontario, with its infinite variety of dramatic scenery, is the showpiece of Canada. Ogdensburg International Bridge stands silhouetted against the sunset at Johnstown *above*. Near Ivy Lea *below right,* the 1,000 Islands International Bridge spans the St Lawrence River. Windsor's beautiful gardens include Dieppe Gardens *above right* and Centennial Park, *centre right* and Hamilton's Royal Botanical Gardens *below* are particularly famous.
The sun sets *left* over spectacular Lake Superior.
International Nickel's mills, smelters and refineries *overleaf* recover 15 elements including nickel, copper, gold and silver.

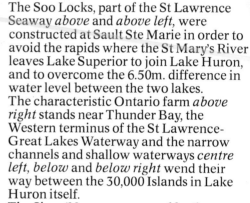

The Soo Locks, part of the St Lawrence Seaway *above* and *above left*, were constructed at Sault Ste Marie in order to avoid the rapids where the St Mary's River leaves Lake Superior to join Lake Huron, and to overcome the 6.50m. difference in water level between the two lakes.
The characteristic Ontario farm *above right* stands near Thunder Bay, the Western terminus of the St Lawrence-Great Lakes Waterway and the narrow channels and shallow waterways *centre left*, *below* and *below right* wend their way between the 30,000 Islands in Lake Huron itself.
The Sioux Narrows, spanned by the slender bridge *below left* form part of the Lake of the Woods, which is divided by the boundary between Canada and the United States whilst in the northeastern corner of the same lake, the rapids *overleaf* are included in the awe-inspiring scenery of the Rushing River Provincial Park.

First published in 1979 by Colour Library International Ltd.
© 1979 Illustrations and text: Colour Library International, 163 East 64th Street, New York 10021.
Colour separations by FERCROM, Barcelona, Spain.
Display and text filmsetting by Focus Photoset, London, England.
Printed and bound by SAGDOS - Brugherio (MI), Italy.
Published by Crescent Books, a division of Crown Publishers Inc.
Library of Congress Catalogue Card No. 79-51713
CRESCENT 1979